In the Name of Jesus

Keith Hubbard

Research Student in Theology, University of Bristol

GROVE BOOKS LIMITED
RIDLEY HALL RD CAMBRIDGE CB3 9HU

Contents

Acknowledgement

I would like to thank the Revd Dr Roland Riem for his sensitive editing of this booklet and for his support.

The Cover Illustration is by Peter Ashton

First Impression February 2000
ISSN 0262-799X
ISBN 1 85174 426 6

1
Introduction

God has reached out to us in Jesus to enable us to come to him in prayer. This booklet plays on this gospel theme to show how, by praying in the name of Jesus, the Father can become enthroned at the heart of human living.

Prayer can require considerable effort on our part amidst life's many distractions and demands. But in Christian prayer the initiative belongs to God. The Holy Spirit within us turns us to God and lifts our prayers before him (Romans 8.26–27). Keeping sight of this big picture—a relationship with God in Christ through the Holy Spirit—should broaden our vision of where praying leads and so help us to relax more into the beauty, truth and goodness of the Father.

The 'Jesus Prayer' provides us with a framework in which to think through the issues more fully. This prayer, in one form or other, has been part of the basic diet for disciples of the Eastern Church for centuries. At its simplest the Prayer is a simple invocation of the name of Jesus. A more formal form is 'Lord Jesus Christ, Son of God, have mercy on me, a sinner,' echoing the cry of the tax collector in Luke 18.13. Each chapter of this booklet will take a word or phrase from this prayer to explore what it means to pray in the name of Jesus. This is not a booklet about the Jesus Prayer as such, but an account of what it means to pray as a Christian, letting the God of Jesus Christ shape our thought and practice.

2
God's Beauty in Jesus: 'Lord'

Prayer to Jesus begins with us confessing that he is Lord—not just our Lord but Lord of all. Even this confession is not our own work but the fruit of God's working in us. The dynamics of prayer must already have reached an advanced stage of development for such utterance of prayer to come about in the first place. Already we must have become helplessly attracted to God's beauty revealed in the face of Jesus Christ. This in turn demonstrates that God has reached out to us and stirred us inwardly to sensitize us to his beauty. This process of coming into relationship with God, in which God's initiative is increasingly realized and enjoyed, takes many forms. Here the relationship can be pictured as God drawing us out of self-involvement and reaching out in his Son, to bring us to a point where we recognize the sovereignty of God in naming Christ as Lord. In such a place we cannot help but acknowledge him to be our own Lord, and indeed at this point we are often overwhelmed by his love.

Beauty has a strong role to play in preparing our hearts to be encountered by God in prayer. What do we usually think of when we think of beauty? The chances are that we do not think of God at first. This is not unusual: we cannot easily imagine beauty in an uncreated realm. We always see it, at least initially, exemplified in beautiful things in the world—a face, a leaf, a building. Beauty is characterized and in a sense defined for us by objects of beauty. We do not carry around with us a yardstick of beauty against which we measure any particular object that we might meet. What is more, our response to beauty is generally immediate. We have no trouble in accounting for the beauty of the world, since it seems to provide its own examples of beauty. But the question remains of how we can conceive of the beauty of God.

The difficulties here are not helped by the fact that beauty has been neglected in much modern Protestant theology. God has more often been seen as holy, a tremendous and fascinating mystery, than as one upon whose face one could look and live, or even love. Beauty has generally been associated with the world, a sign of God's unutterable glory. So long as the discussion takes place on the level of concepts, we are unlikely to make much headway. This is because beauty is not something one can turn into an objective and unchanging property; it has always to do with how an object is perceived or experienced. Even a building is beautiful only in relation to light or shade or to the shifting viewpoint of an occupant. So long as theology tried to pin down God's properties from the outside by reason alone it was bound to overlook the beauty of God.

In prayer we begin to find something analogous to the experience of beauty, and the language of beauty begins to become appropriate to describe God. In practice, especially in worship, aesthetic and spiritual experience often appear to be inseparable from one another, although it is very important not to confuse the two things. When we are encountered by God in prayer then often one of the first characteristics will be what we might call spiritual or charismatic experience. This can play an important role in leading us on to a deeper level of prayerful relationship in many different ways, although it is a common mistake to think that such experience belongs only to an early stage of prayer. It should accompany us every step of the way.

One of the ways in which such experience is aroused is in a sense of indescribable sweetness being poured out in the heart of the one praying. This can be felt almost like honey which, remaining upon the lips at first, can then be traced to the region of the heart. The heart is, as it were, the place where our relationship with God flourishes as we invoke Jesus' name. Prayer is working one of its many transformations in our relationship with God. No longer is this relationship simply a verbal exchange (the primary medium of many everyday relationships) but heart-to-heart. This praying relationship touches the heart, where we are most vulnerable and which consequently we try to keep hidden. Addressing God as Lord can seem rather like any other conversation, in which we expect to keep certain prerogatives. But whenever prayer descends from the lips to the heart it reaches a more intimate place, where God is able to surprise, delight and jolt us away from any desire we might have to keep control.

We are not of course to pray for the sake of having such experiences of sweetness, and indeed we cannot. That would then not be prayer but something else. The point is that, though the depths God's glory are inaccessible to us (1 Tim 6.16), the beauty of the Father that is eternally enjoyed by and reflected in the Son is translated by the Spirit into forms that we ourselves are able to enjoy. This is what Jesus allows us to glimpse in prayer through a willingness, which is also of his making, to be open to what is both beautiful and spiritual. God has then, as we pray, stirred our heart and opened it up so that it has become able to catch a glimpse of the beauty of the Lord.

The Desire for Intimacy

Even a glimpse provides light enough for us to see that our own heart is attuned to who God is. We can no longer rest. We are not content with the beauty of the world, even though our having been encountered by God may also revive our aesthetic experience. We have tasted of the beauty of Jesus and we are now filled with an unquenchable thirst for more of Jesus. Invocation of the name of Jesus can therefore never be a single event. It is necessarily repeated because part of what it means to call upon Jesus is to desire more and more of his closeness and to experience more and more of his beauty. It is not uncommon for people who have been caught up in the presence of the Lord to utter 'Jesus' constantly and indeed helplessly.

Often such passion characterizes the awakening of our call to Christian ministry of some kind. It is a shame when such a sense of our intimacy with Jesus becomes lost in the practice of the ministry itself and is ascribed only to the early stages of spirituality. Such intimacy invariably contributes an endless vitality to Christian thought and practice in whatever forms it takes. The contemporary prophet Paul Cain, speaking at a conference in London back in 1990, has this to say:

We just cannot say enough about intimacy [with Jesus]. When I was a little boy I fell so insatiably in love with Jesus that I used to slip out of my bed at three or four o'clock in the morning, and I would go out into a lonely deserted field out in the country and I would hide there between the high stalks of corn or whatever was growing, and I would just call out the name of Jesus and adore him and tell him how much I loved him and ask him to speak to me. And I fell in love with the name of Jesus.

One rarely hears testimonies of such passion in the church today. Indeed the place of giving testimonies in church has generally become less prominent, even in charismatic churches. In the charismatic movement there has been much emphasis throughout the last ten years on our need to prepare for revival. If we could cry out to God with the quality of passion being demonstrated here by Paul Cain, and express such passion openly, then we would perhaps be in the position of being able to respond to God's desire to visit the church with revival.

3

God's Mission in the Name: 'Jesus'

In the last chapter we saw that calling upon the name of the Lord is a fitting response to God's communication of his beauty in Jesus. Now we focus more definitely on the significance of Jesus' name for Christian mission. Sometimes it is argued that, because God became incarnate in Jesus at a particular time and place, mission cannot be carried out in Jesus' name in other cultures whose time and place have little in common with his situation. This chapter therefore considers our affirmation that it is in the name of Jesus, and no other, that we must be saved (Acts 4.12). It also considers the temporal character of mission and how the Jesus Prayer is helpful in moving us away from temporal experiences that are a distraction from our participation in God's mission in the world.

We began the last chapter by noting that calling upon Jesus in prayer already says something about the place of Jesus in our lives. The grace of God has already brought us to a place where prayer is possible. This grace is at work outside the little stretches of time that we deliberately devote to praying. Similarly, invocation of the name involves more than simply uttering the word 'Jesus.' It requires a certain degree of harmony between the one being called and the expectations of the one doing the calling. In other words, Jesus is only named as Jesus when he already occupies a certain place in a person's life. This need not imply that that person is a Christian who holds to the doctrines and practices of a particular church. Nor does it mean that there is some magic cord extending between the word 'Jesus' and the living person to whom that word refers, as if a tug on the cord might instantly bring Jesus' presence to someone. The naming of Jesus always entails a real reaching out of the heart in the grace of the Holy Spirit.

The fact that Jesus cannot be proclaimed Lord without the Holy Spirit (1 Cor 12.3) again distinguishes the name of Jesus from mere words such as 'Jesus' and 'Lord,' since these can clearly be abused in all sorts of ways irrespective of the presence of the Holy Spirit. Although it is occasionally said that it is arrogant to maintain that Jesus' name is the only one in which we must be saved, this is at least in part a confusion between the word 'Jesus' and the one to whom the word points. It is clearly possible to be known by Jesus, and to respond to this in a transforming way, independently of whether a person uses such a word or not. The faith of people with severe learning difficulties would be one example. Acknowledging this possibility only serves to magnify the saving power of the name of Jesus.

We should therefore be bold in affirming that only in Jesus can we be reconciled to God and brought into the fullness of intimacy with him, which he has prepared for us all. But of course, although we are not simply to equate the word 'Jesus' with the name of Jesus, this does not mean that those who use it in prayer will be ignored! The word carries the same potential for naming him as it did in his earthly ministry. There is thus a certain privilege to be accorded even the word 'Jesus,' although non-Christian cultures are not thereby bereft.

The powerful claim of the hymn in Philippians 2 is that at the name of Jesus 'every knee should bend' (Phil 2.10). This universal claim means that no human being upon recognizing Jesus for who he is (which I believe all will have to do at some point) will be able to refrain from glorifying him as Lord. The term 'Lord' in this wonderful hymn conveys this universal event of the recognition of Jesus' identity as divine. It attests that the language with which we properly glorify God is equally applicable to Jesus. The outward form of the term does not matter but the dynamics of one's relationship with God in Jesus. If we keep this distinction in mind we can see how repeating the name of Jesus in prayer—voicing 'Jesus' in the context of a living faith—is the very essence of the Jesus Prayer, bringing us into Jesus' proximity.

Being close to Jesus brings a taste of eternity to the one praying, but not at the expense of a life in time. Rather we come to relate to time in a different way, from a different perspective that has to do sharing in God's work. We are not merely held in a warm embrace in the name of Jesus but also drawn into a transformative relationship with him, in which we come to see the world of time more and more through his eyes. There is a movement outward and to others that starts, as it were, with a movement upwards—a cry of the heart to the Lord Jesus. We become prepared for a life in time by being distanced from the everyday patterns of our own temporal existence. And in adjusting to the value of God who is other than ourselves, we become better able to spend time with those whose values are other than our own. This movement into time makes us aware again of our need for God, so we can be sent out again in his name. The dynamic of the Jesus Prayer suggests how we might live in time for the sake of mission, for in such prayer we are sent onward and out by the one we are invoking.

Reckoning Time

The repeated use of the name of Jesus can transform our relationship to time in other ways. Citizens of the modern world cannot escape having lives that are in some sense based upon the clock. We get up at a certain time and do things at various discrete points in the day. The ticking of the clock suggests that every second is similarly defined, each second measuring out an identical period to the last. There is nothing in the clock to indicate that one second should be qualitatively different from any other. And there is clearly a part of us that finds this formal reckoning of time conducive to our own lifestyle. This sort of time is like a piece of cloth that we are able to cut up in various ways, a resource for our own use. We set aside a time for work, a 'quality time' for family and a 'quiet time' for God. But in so doing we are in danger of making ourselves responsible for arranging the shape of our lives, rather than allowing openness to God's initiative to prevail.

Repetition could be seen as the structural tissue of time, because repetition of what has gone before forms the basis of our sense of the rhythm and pace of time. The incessant ticking of the clock is one potent symbol of this. Yet the repetition of the Jesus Prayer has a different meaning, in that it is not susceptible to being structured by our own intentions. Each utterance is not simply another instance of the one preceding it, but represents a step forward in our journey with God. With each step we gain encouragement from God leading us onwards and we are dependent upon him. This is of value in helping us to sense that our time is not our own but belongs to God. Time is not in fact stuff at our disposal, nor even a neutral framework in which we play out our lives; time is the expression of God's dealings with the world. When God gives himself to the world, time is what it takes. It is this endless self-giving in time that, as we shall see more and more, calls forth a like response from our own heart.

The repeating of the name of Jesus therefore opens up another possibility for transformation: we give up to God our propensity to be the Lord of our own time and we put 'our' time into God's hands for the sake of his mission. We ourselves become God's hands in our identification with God's missionary purposes in his Word and his Spirit.

4

God's Truth in Jesus: 'Christ'

In the last chapter we saw how we give up to God in prayer the timing of our own projects in order that our interests may coincide with those of God more perfectly. We no longer conceive of ourselves as embarking upon a mission; rather we are appointed agents in God's own mission. What this mission is will clearly be bound together with our view of what counts for truth.

This chapter attempts to describe how Jesus as the truth shapes us in prayer, so that when we go out in his name we go out in the name of truth. This is obviously a dangerous assertion, given that historically mission has often left a trail of physical and cultural destruction in its wake. I want to stress, therefore, how the living truth we meet in prayer is intended for the anointing of the world with mercy.

In prayer the agency of the one praying can become so completely surrendered to God that the Holy Spirit can take the divine mission deeply into the heart of the one praying. This is another sign of our known selves becoming decentred. What we know and do, even what we are, is transformed as we enter the depths of our relationship with Christ. In him we outgrow a disposition of self-assertion and grow into one of fundamental receptivity to the mission of the Spirit. In the case of the Jesus Prayer, this reversal can be experienced in a fairly literal way. In time it is possible to become aware of the prayer being continuously repeated in one's heart, independently of one's conscious intentions to utter it. The voice of the Holy Spirit can be smothered by worldly concerns but it is not the world itself that prevents the Spirit from acting. The Spirit is only quenched when the one praying acts out of step with the divine passion for the world.

In this reversal of orientation, where it is no longer a case of us actively praying to God but of God praying in us, we need to discover a new conception of truth. The Christian's answer to the question 'What is truth?' must necessarily be different from that of others because here truth is Christ himself. Truth is bound up with the second person of the Trinity who communicates and embodies the truth of God. For the Christian, truth is not essentially a property of propositions like 'grass is green,' nor is it a property of a person, even of Jesus. Jesus did not merely say 'I am truthful' or 'My words are true.' He said 'I am the truth' (John 14.6). This has radical implications for the way in which truth is to be defined, discussed and lived.

Of course we do not normally treat truth as if it were something you could parcel up in a proposition, as if the truth of assertions is all that concerns us. In fact, when we pay close attention to the way in which language is used in everyday situations, the truth of persons seems more fundamental. People are not ultimately concerned with whether assertion are true or not—though in particular cases this is obviously important—but with whether the person making the assertions is true. Furthermore, we call many expressions of a person's life true that could simply not be translated into propositional form: character and attitude, thoughts and feelings, intuitions and hunches. On the one hand, the truth of particular claims is mostly used to establish the integrity of the person. And on the other hand what we know of such integrity is remembered to judge whether what is being talked about is worthy of attention. What we value in a person is their integrity, whereas we can overlook them making a certain number of erroneous claims, provided they are made in good faith.

Furthermore, we commonly refer to people as being true or false in contexts where what they have said is not at issue. We might well allow that what a person has said is true and yet remain concerned that the person herself is not. This happens in cases where there is reason to suppose that someone's motives for saying something are at variance with the context of what is being said. Whether a person is deemed true or not will depend on more subtle things such as how ready he is to be swept along by the tide of current opinion. Readiness to go along with and act upon a partial truth, without taking the trouble to evaluate it, can be more indicative of a person's falsity than any incorrect assertion. Not to protest against a lie can be as much an expression of falsity as simply to utter the lie in the first place.

True Disclosure

Truth and falsity are clearly already at work at a personal level before any assertions have been made. Truth may be said to consist in the capacity of persons to remember or represent things aright. When one has discovered for oneself the genuine character of something then one has taken it out of hiding, or the realm in which its value has been forgotten, and has set forth its truth. Knowing the truth is a process of personal discovery and re-evaluation. The sense of the New Testament word for truth (*aletheia*) also suggests this. The stem is the word for forgetfulness or hiddenness, *lethe*. In the Greek mythic worldview the river Lethe, which led to the land of the dead, would carry away the memories of the deceased so that they might forget their former lives. The prefix 'a-' implies that truth resides in un-forgetfulness (remembering) or un-covering (discovering). Hence the classical understanding of truth associates it with discovery. Truth is in the nature of persons and has to do with the integrity of their life among other persons.

When we turn to Christ in prayer we are turning to the one who embodied truth, whose whole life enacted a discovery of a realm that had been hidden—the kingdom of God. And yet this truth never becomes impersonal. It is offered in human encounter through the agency of the Christ, the one anointed by God's Spirit, and received by turning in faith towards the one who is and was and is to come. This is the movement of the Jesus Prayer. In confessing the name of Christ we are freed by the truth of Jesus to live in love for others, no longer subject to our own unaided moral dispositions or fixed religious ideologies.

We can only open our heart to facilitate our receptivity to such truth, and accordingly we have to give up our own desires to establish the truth for ourselves. Jesus alone is to be identified with the truth and is the source of all truth. Truth for the Christian therefore has more the character of revelation than discovery. We cannot uncover the things of the Spirit of our own initiative. Rather, the Holy Spirit reveals them step by step as we too live in the truth of Christ.

Ultimately Jesus reveals our true selves to ourselves in prayer, as those wholly known and loved by God. The Jesus Prayer facilitates this by separating the conscious intentions of the one praying from their expression. Thus the prayer can be maintained even in sleep, being perpetuated by the Holy Spirit. The prayer disarms us of our control over our intentions and subjects us to the fact that the truth of God is to be revealed to us by intentions beyond our own. The Holy Spirit, who leads us into all truth (John 16.13) shows us that truth is to be disclosed to us only in Jesus' name. And in this name we are invigorated and sent out to be effective channels of God's love in his mission in the world.

5

God's Goodness in Jesus: 'Son of God'

In the last chapter we attempted to describe how Christians come to conceive of truth differently through their prayer in the Spirit. The quest to discover truth as something to be asserted is supplanted by a humble acceptance of the revelation of truth given in the face of Jesus Christ. In this chapter we shall see how this has prepared us for a similar reversal concerning the nature of goodness.

When we proclaim things like 'God is good' what we mean is that God is good in a way analogous to the ways in which virtuous people are good, only at a higher level. To put it more philosophically, there is continuity between ascriptions of value to God and everyday value-claims. Indeed this is partly what offers any possibility of speaking of a God who is beyond all human definition. Yet we should note that this approach assumes that goodness may be adequately defined independently of God. Goodness can be recognized in others independently of any comparisons with the being of God.

We could argue, however, that value-expressing language might be even more comprehensively understood the other way around, as being dependent upon a concept of God. God then represents the absolute standard of goodness against which all talk of good can be measured. As we said earlier concerning truth, attention to how language is used reveals that we do in fact use terms as if they reflect something of the nature of God. As for truth so for goodness. A good action is an unselfish one; and the reason for this is that it reflects something of the self-giving nature of God. The fact that we quite naturally value efforts to overcome selfishness cannot be accounted for only in terms of the public benefits of this attitude. We are inherently orientated in such a way that we knowingly aspire toward self-giving; and this distinguishes us from other mammals in an important respect. We are essentially ethical in our being and this can best be accounted for in terms of the ends for which God created us.

To be made in God's image is to participate to some extent in his nature of self-giving. Such self-giving is therefore basic to our existence and runs against the impulses of our self-interest. A self-giving nature is common to all. But a Christian is someone whose own natural (and flawed) propensity for self-giving has been caught up into God's eternal activity of self-emptying in Christ and who lives his or her life in emulation of the fulfilment of this activity in Jesus' life and death.

This implies that our understanding of goodness—like our understanding

13

of truth and beauty—is to be based upon our understanding of the nature of God as exemplified in Jesus. We must focus upon the meaning of God's self-emptying of his goodness if we are to understand the way in which this may be enacted in everyday life. Then we will value goodness not simply in itself but also as something that participates in the nature of God. Here is another reversal for us: things are good not primarily because they satisfy our own criteria of goodness or that of our society, but because they reflect the goodness of God's being as one of endless giving.

Again the Jesus Prayer helps us to understand the way in which goodness—like truth and beauty—is to be authentically comprehended only in Jesus. The designation of Jesus as the Son of God points us to his relations with God as Son of the Father, by whom he is sent into the world in the communion of Holy Spirit. Thus God's goodness can be seen as a fullness, a Trinitarian event, which is dynamic and inexhaustibly full of love.

Dynamic Goodness

We can expand on this theme of goodness in God. In the first centuries of the life of the church Christians came to see that God's life was richer than had ever been appreciated before the coming of Christ and the outpouring of the Holy Spirit. They came to understand on the basis of their experience and the testimony of the Scriptures that God's life is characterized by what is given and received abundantly among the persons of the Trinity. 'What can be given when each is divine?' is a fair question, to which Christians can answer that divinity is not a stuff that is contained in equal measure by separable beings; divinity is in inter-relationship. The persons of the Trinity are distinct but distinguished precisely in their relationships with each other. Divinity is an energetic but patterned, overflowing but balanced, flux of mutuality between persons. This would be a contemporary exposition of the biblical phrase 'God is love,' and its importance lies in the dynamism it injects into the notion of goodness.

God's goodness in the Son of God from eternity consists in his being sent from the Father and receiving sonship in the Spirit to return to the Father. This energy is given to the world in the incarnation of the Son. All this mutuality, this absolute reciprocity of relationship is given to the world in the sending of the Son. His mission is to be the firstborn among many brothers, to be the firstfruits of new creation, to draw the world into the goodness of God. His goodness and loving purposes for the world are one.

Just as God's love is dynamic it is also inexhaustible. Love is what constitutes God's very existence. Turned outwards towards the world it is ever abundant, ever intent to give itself to the other, ever reaching out to the other. Love compels God to reach out to the world, giving it a profusion of life, in order to generate as many means as possible by which his love may be shared.

14

It is love that compels God to throw the net of possible relationships with himself as wide as can be. God's love, then, is a giving of nothing less than his being, since his being is love. In everyday discourse we refer to sending in cases where a gift is given that leaves the sender independent of the recipient. In Christ, however, there are no such distinctions: the one giving gives of himself and is even defined in terms of this self-sending character. God retains the dignity of the one and only Father by divesting himself, pouring himself out in his Son in an incomparable act of self-emptying.

In such a movement of outpouring, God gives of himself without reserve and demonstrates his inexhaustible goodness. To hold anything back would contradict the fact that it is the same love involved in creation that also defines himself. There is thus an identity between the way God's being is expressed toward the world and toward himself. This self-emptying character of God's love is shown to us again and again in acts of goodness: in the foundational self-emptying of the Son of God in the incarnation (Phil 2.7); in the pouring out of his precious blood in the eucharistic wine (Matt 26.28); in God's pouring out of himself in his death, symbolized by the blood and water that poured from Jesus' side on the cross (John 19.34); in Christ's pouring out of the Holy Spirit at Pentecost for the empowerment of us all for mission (Acts 2.33); and in the pouring out of the church in sacrificial emulation of Jesus' example and inspired by the Spirit (Phil 2.17).

Decanting the Life of God

There is therefore a multi-layered and deep decanting of the life of God for the sake of the world. This is God's goodness in all its fullness. God the source of all goodness is never diminished or exhausted in this giving. This would contradict the fact that God is infinite, for then his being would be defined by a finite measure of love. Rather God's love is endless and superabundant, always giving more than it is possible for the world to receive. It is therefore inconceivable for the eternal being of God to be fully received by the temporal being of the world. Indeed, God's self-emptying is also a self-replenishing from the perspective of the world, as his gift to the world draws the world glorified into his fullness.

The one who prays to the Son of God stands before One who is prepared to pour himself into each particular creature, loving each uniquely, to raise that creature into his abundant life. However much the heart expands to make room for goodness there is always more to receive. God is the Supreme Good, a new wine bursting old wineskins. This means that there is no end of goodness to those who live by the Spirit of the Son. The crucifixion of Christ is a vivid demonstration that even the cup of suffering and death become a cup of blessing poured out for others when the heart is filled full with God's goodness.

6
God's Reaching Out in Jesus: 'Have Mercy'

We have so far seen how prayer brings about a reversal of orientation in our relationships with one another, the world and God. We can leave behind the need to guard ourselves or to seek life through others and become more able to find fulfilment in genuine mutuality. We come to be more patient and dependent upon God for all things and desire to share what we have with others. In short, we come to be more and more like God in prayer.

The receptivity called for to allow such inner changes does raise questions about how best to see prayer. It is far more than a chat between friends, however helpful telephone imagery may be for children. Prayer is primarily God reaching out in communication with us. An emphasis on reaching out, therefore, might better inform the practice of prayer. Generally we reach out for an object of some kind only when we have the confidence so to do. When we have become disorientated in ourselves, we are only capable of reaching out blindly and helplessly. The baby reaches out for its mother's breast whether it is available or not.

Our propensity to reach out for something is a vital human disposition. In reaching out we assume the existence of something other than ourselves, even though we do not always find the object which we are seeking. Reaching out not only assumes that the object sought exists but is of value. When we reach out for something we have already grasped hold of it at some level. When I reach out for my pen, for example, I do so without needing to reflect upon what I am doing. I do not pause to consider that the pen might not be what I have always taken it to be. To reach out for an object of ordinary experience implies a relationship that issues in practical activity. It is only when something goes wrong—the pen is broken—that the automatic manner of reaching out for the pen is disturbed. What should I do? Do I go out and buy a new pen, and if so with what kind of pen should I replace the old one? Do I continue to look for it, only no longer with such immediate confidence that I will be successful in obtaining what I am reaching out for? The absence of the pen somehow brings it into being for us.

True prayer is perhaps more analogous to our flailing attempts to reach out for an absent object than being able to pick something up directly. We assume that we are reaching out to God in prayer, and that he is really there. We may even use various formulas of expression to ensure that we are addressing the correct object, the 'God and Father of Jesus Christ,' and so on. But too often it may feel like we are reaching out for an object easily within our grasp. The character that this prayer takes is like something upon which we have already decided. Our prayer becomes automatic, and jaded. It is only when the network of our relationships comes unstuck that our reaching out becomes also a crying out to God, as the baby cries for its mother. In times of sickness, for example, when we are incapable of doing anything much and can no longer reach out for familiar objects, we are thrown back upon our isolation. You cry out for God, helpless like a child. Is he there for you? This is a moment of true prayer.

At such times we are no longer conceiving of God in any way comparable to an object of experience. We do not pray to him for his blessing on this or that project, though we may well pray for health. Yet it is precisely in such moments that God's presence comes to us. God's presence coincides with the very absence of God in the world that we have tried to arrange carefully around ourselves.

God is like the mother who cannot help but immediately respond to the cry of her child. She cannot act otherwise, or refrain from acting. Then we realize that there is something of peculiar value here that we desire to hold close to us. We have not been speaking at, to or of God—we have simply cried out, not reaching out in any definite or articulate way. At this point prayer has been permitted to take on a whole new meaning. We have given up on prayer as an initiative of our own design, on prayer as finding a tidy place in our working life, almost like a clear space on the desk. We can no longer grasp God by our own efforts; rather we allow ourselves to be found by God and searched by God; and finally we know ourselves to be known by God.

In crying out we become aware that we can never know God in any sense that we could conceive by reason. We realize that we cannot reach out to God in any way that could give another the impression that we knew precisely what we were doing. God comes to us, searches us, convicts us. In this we know God's mercy: a knowing that we are known by God and—in the face of our helplessness and nothingness—are accepted and loved by him.

7

God's Conviction in Jesus: 'Upon Me'

In the last chapter we moved from our reaching out to God to our being found and searched by God; but we could only come to this by passing through a crying out for God. We found that such crying out is often voiced in contexts where one becomes somehow cut off from our everyday world. Of course when we become ill, family and friends often come to our aid and we can know God's love in their tending. I have, however, been concentrating on an interior movement where God's mercy is experienced immediately as an undeserved presence.

I would claim not only that it is right for us to enjoy a personal and inward relationship with God, but that significant aspects of our overall life with God and one another are to be nurtured here. Such inwardness has its own energy which in time turns us outwards again into the world, where our activities and relationships are invested with meaning and colour.

Let us take the example of reconciliation. A beautiful example of this can be found in David Lynch's recent and sensitive film about old age, *The Straight Story*. This is based upon the real life story of a seventy-three-year-old man from Iowa called Alvin Straight. After hearing that his brother has had a stroke and also realizing that he himself might not have long to live, he prepares himself to travel the three hundred miles to see him by his only means of transport, a lawnmower. The point is that Straight's consciousness of their impending death makes him determined to see his brother, to whom he has not spoken for a decade, and be reconciled to him. The reconciliation seems to be brought about when the brother realizes that Straight has been travelling for months on end on a lawnmower just to see him.

When we ask for the mercy of Jesus Christ to fall upon us we do so from a sense of our own human mortality and frailty. It is a personal, but never individualistic, confession of need as we make it in solidarity with the entire human race. But more directly, this awareness of finitude brings to the fore those things that are of final value to us—things that we could not face death without having done something about—and speaks to us of the possibility of setting ourselves at rest about them. It provides us with a horizon of what is genuinely possible for us still to do and which should be done. Often this may be accompanied by a sense of regret for not having done such things earlier, just as Alvin Straight seems in the film to carry about with him a need to make up for the previous ten years with his brother, years that seem to trundle behind him like the trailer of his lawnmower.

Awareness of human frailty therefore is not introspective. It inevitably takes us out of ourselves in practical accountability to others. This is especially true of families and communities. Alvin Straight's awareness of his own failure to 'make peace' earlier with his brother issues in advice he gives to others at various points in the film, that they should affirm the other members of their own families and let them know that they are valued. Especially moving is a scene set around an open fire of burning sticks, where he attempts to console a girl who has run away from her family, believing that they would reject her for becoming pregnant. His words to her are as follows:

> When my kids were little I used to play a game with them. I would give each of them a stick, one for each one of them, and I would say 'You break that'—and of course they could, real easy. Then I would say 'Tie them sticks in a bundle and try to break that'—and of course they could not. Then I would say 'That bundle, that's family.'

The perennial wisdom being expressed here summarizes the sense in which an individual's integrity can only be found in relationship, in community. It is no accident that this same basic metaphor for family and friendship can be found throughout history. It is witnessed in Ecclesiastes 4.9–16, a saying of which, recorded in v 12, provides a specific parallel to Straight's words of wisdom: 'a threefold cord is not quickly broken.' Interestingly, this saying may also be found in the much earlier Sumerian body of epic literature that presumably fed into this OT tradition. It expresses a truth at the heart of any social structure and a truth inhabited by anyone who confesses his or her radical incompleteness without God and the people of God.

Our true identity is only to be found in the family of God—the church. Yet God's love is never lost in a crowd. He does not deal with us *en bloc*, as a member of a collective, but rather as persons, each held in being in relation to others by his love. Far from being cogs in an ecclesiastical machine, his love and concern for each of us is a necessary condition for the church to be a united and diverse body in which people flourish as themselves. Our integrity is to be found in our filial and ecclesial relationships as members of the growing body of Christ.

In prayer God deals with us individually, as uniquely loved members of his household of faith. He takes us into his heart so that we may know ourselves to be objects of his mercy and of infinite importance to him. This is the opposite of individualism because it implies the resignation of our first person perspective and the welcoming of God's universal love. We become 'me' rather than 'I', the object of love rather than the subject of choosing, the one with whom God is dealing mercifully. As that 'me' becomes our core identity we become able to live out that identity among others, giving them the freedom from having to fulfil our need for security.

8

God's Grace in Jesus: 'A Sinner'

Often this phrase of the Jesus prayer is omitted, and in a sense it only reinforces what we have already begun to say about the identity of a praying person. Certainly 'sinner' is a name we truthfully call ourselves. As Paul says, 'all have sinned and fall short of the glory of God' (Romans 3.23). It would be fair to say, however, that in the Eastern Church the identity of a sinner has always been seen as a cause for hope, even celebration, because it puts us in a place before God where we can be justified. Remember that the Jesus Prayer is essentially the prayer of Luke's tax-collector.

As we name ourselves sinners, our need for God's mercy is at once transparent to us. We realize that we are created out of nothing, and that we will return to nothing without the grace of God working within us. Our culture encourages its people to construct their self-identity through seeking possessions or status, but this illusion can be broken by the deliberate effort to dethrone the self. Having retracted our gaze from our preoccupations in the world, we are able to penetrate their vanity and realize that our fundamental identity cannot come from ourselves. We come to realize that all value—including any good that we may appear to do or that is ascribed to us in public—must be ascribed to the mercy of Jesus dwelling within us.

Our struggle to come to simplicity of heart reminds us that sin still overshadows our heart. Yet this is not a cause of despair but renewed honesty in prayer. If the possibility of maintaining our own purity of heart belonged to us, then we might become an object of God's love but not of his mercy. Only in Jesus do we become an object of God's merciful love, and only in Jesus may we attain purity of heart. The penitential character of the Jesus Prayer means that we need not always make the confession 'a sinner' explicit. Only those who already know themselves to be sinners can begin to utter the prayer with conviction, although their sense of sinfulness may deepen as does their sense of being in receipt of God's overwhelming grace.

When the Jesus Prayer is used in practice this last phrase is often left unspoken. However, while it is true that this phrase is implied by what has come before, it clearly has an expressive value on the lips of the one who prays. It is precisely this sense of sinfulness that compels us to come back to the Lord in repentance and faith to cry out again 'Lord Jesus' and reiterate the Jesus Prayer again and again.

Once we have recognized our nothingness before God this prepares us for fresh insight into the gracious character of our relationship to God. We see that we have been trying to make ourselves a place in the world that is altogether too cosy. Our mind has been pre-occupied with small circles of reasoning, enough for survival in a busy and complex world. Even such a simple thought as 'Why is my pen missing?' might issue in a series of attempts to account for the fact of the pen being absent. 'Did I leave it in the other room?' 'Did someone borrow it?' None of these questions is useless in itself, but they come to nothing when they flurry from an agitated and untranquil mind. In prayer, dissipating habits of thought can be broken as the mind comes to rest in the graciousness of God.

'Why did he choose me?' There is no reason. You are unable to account for the fact that you exist, for the fact that you are at this moment being held in being by God. The situation is not subject to your decision any more than a child should decide to be born. You know that God 'searches hearts and minds': your heart and your mind (Rev 2.23). You know yourself to be searched by God and that perhaps it is already only an expression of his mercy that you are able to respond to him at all. You dare to cry out to Jesus 'have mercy on me, a sinner.' And we discover, though it defies reason, that precisely in acknowledging our nothingness before God we find God's merciful love poured out afresh in our heart.

In prayer our hearts echo the theme of St Paul: 'the grace of our Lord overflowed for me' (1 Tim 1.14). Grace lies outside our control, though never outside God's; grace is nothing other than the hand of God at work. God's Spirit searches our heart, tending it with the utmost care, like a gardener not wanting to disturb the new shoots of spring as he removes some weeds from around them. Just as each flower in a garden is unique, so we know ourselves to be unique to God as he reaches through the many recesses of our heart.

Confessing that one is a sinner is a vital, but never a final, part of praying. It is indeed frightening to admit that one is radically unfinished and in danger of being unmade but, as Luke reminds us, the point of admitting one's lostness is the joy of being found and coming home to God (Luke 15.7). As we have said, the Jesus Prayer is meant for repetition—'sinner' is never given the last word but is always the gateway for the Lord to re-enter with beauty, truth and goodness, bringing new blessedness to those who know their need of God.

9
Concluding Reflections

In this booklet I have tried to address some images of ourselves in relation to God which may be deficient and which may consequently hinder us as we face God in prayer. I have not delved into the philosophical background of our culture but its legacy is discernible in our assumptions about how to pray. We see ourselves as independent people who can come to grasp what God is like through conversation with him. However, our focus has been on God knowing us rather than on our having knowledge of God or even knowing him. This is consistent with biblical theology. True love is to be defined not in terms of the love we may have for God but in terms of God's love for us in Jesus (1 John 4.10).

Though this may sound strange, I have never wanted to know God, at least in the conditions of this life, as much as I have grown in my desire to be known by God (see Gal 4.9, 1 Cor 13.12). Yet acknowledging this does not lead me to vagueness about what God is like and whether he exists. The process of prayer as I have described it brings one into an overwhelming sense of the existence of God, so great that we cease to define our place in the world by our own means and can even come to affirm our nothingness as creatures. We turn back to the world with our existence affirmed in a fresh way, for we know it grounded upon God's own existence and held in being by his mercy.

To know oneself to be known by God, indeed, to know the depth of God's love, does not tally with seeing God as an object of knowledge. Throughout this booklet we have had to adapt common parlance to fit the ways in which God chooses to relate to us. Frequently this has involved a reversal of perspective to do justice to the dynamics of prayer. But as it is not just prayer that is done in the name of Jesus, I would like to end by briefly raising some implications for practical ministries such as evangelism, preaching and spirituality.

Traditional modes of evangelism have tended to distinguish at once between those who know God and those who do not. This separates one set of people from the other and creates a situation where one group is 'in' with God and the other 'out.' This can cause resentment among those who are being evangelized as they see those who claim to know God in a way they do not as smug and self-righteous. Problems like this inevitably arise when one takes a first person perspective as a basis for describing different relationships people might have to God. On the other hand, one can hardly claim that God knows some people more than others. He knows us all inside out, and he loves us all equally. The pressing difference is that Christians have a vivid awareness of God's searching knowledge of their own heart as they call upon his name in Jesus, whereas others lack this. I want others to know themselves to be searched through and through by God, and to see that they can never begin to know the reaches of their own heart otherwise. It is this that motivates me to talk to others about Jesus.

The same applies to preaching, insofar as preaching attempts to convey knowledge of God and to communicate the value of this knowledge to others. In doing this the preacher may appear to be characterizing himself as a knowing subject—or as one gifted with knowledge of which others are ignorant—rather than pointing to God as the source of all knowing. A bad preacher is someone who points to himself as a subject of interest and a source of truth. A good preacher by contrast is someone who refers to himself only as a means of communicating the mercy of Jesus. There has been much emphasis on story-telling in recent years—whereas people used to give 'testimonies' they now relate their 'stories.' The terminology is unimportant so long as the essence of testimony is preserved. This consists in giving particular accounts of events in which Jesus' name is glorified, in using such events in order to 'confess that Jesus Christ is Lord' (Phil 2.11). This then can become the seedbed of evangelism and also prophecy (Rev 19.19).

Finally, we might reflect that spirituality is sometimes discussed in terms of knowing, doing and being, with each strand given varying emphasis according to whose spirituality is being discussed. For example, liberationists tend to stress the doing, evangelicals the knowing and contemplatives the being. What tends to characterize such discussions however is the anthropological manner in which such categories are defined. Our age has often put the emphasis on being, as if somehow our attempts to rediscover the relative importance of being could provide the basis for an appropriate Christian spirituality. In contrast to this we might say that spirituality is not about our own doing or knowing, nor even our being; it is rather about being known, met and led by God in his activity of reaching out to every particle of his creation.

The Jesus Prayer is not a cure-all for the misperceptions that beset our efforts to evangelize, preach, and develop our spirituality. But it can at least open up the possibility that by praying in a Trinitarian pattern we, and the ministries in which we share, will be conformed to the one to whom we pray, to the glory of his name.